# TEMPERATE
## FOREST HABITATS

*BY*
### BARBARA TAYLOR

# THE LIVING FOREST

Temperate woodlands are beautiful places that are mainly found in the northern hemisphere. Temperate woodlands are made up of two different types – cold coniferous forests in the south and warmer deciduous forests in the north. They are very different from tropical climates because they are affected by the seasons. Tropical forests are hot and wet all year round, with plenty of food always available. But in temperate forests, plants and animals have to survive changes in the weather, especially the cold winter season. The woodland trees provide food and shelter for many different birds, mammals, insects and other creatures. Lots of plants and fungi thrive in rich woodland soils. Yet large areas of woodlands, particularly deciduous forests, have been destroyed for their timber, or cleared to make way for farms or towns.

## WOODLAND TYPES

There are two main types of temperate forests: the dark, cold coniferous woods and the warmer, lighter deciduous forests. Sometimes the wooded areas are a mixture of these two woodland types (left). Deciduous trees lose their leaves at the end of their growing season and coniferous trees keep their leaves all year round.

## AUSTRALIAN TEMPERATE FORESTS

The honey possum lives in the eucalyptus woodlands of Australia. The honey possum, parrots and bats all feed on eucalyptus trees and shrubs. As the creatures eat, they pollinate the plants,

which makes the seeds develop. The honey possum's long, thin tongue is tipped with bristles to help it eat.

## SEASONAL SLEEP

Like some other woodland animals, dormice survive the cold winter by hibernating, which is like a long sleep. During the hibernation the dormice save energy by slowing their hearts down. A hibernating dormouse lives off fat stored in its body after it has eaten as much as it can in the autumn. Every now and then the dormouse wakes up, is active for a few days, and then goes back into hibernation. If a winter is too mild a dormouse can wake up too often and lose too much energy.

## EXPERT CLIMBER

Many woodland animals need to be good climbers so they can find food and places to nest, as well as to escape from predators. Squirrels have strong back legs and sharp claws to climb trees quickly. They can climb down trees head first because their feet turn outwards at the ankle. A bushy
il helps them to keep their balance as they
ıp from branch to branch.

## NESTING PLACES

From tree holes and branches to piles of leaves on the ground, woodlands are full of nesting places for birds. The wood warbler builds its nest on the ground with grass to keep the eggs and chicks warm. Wood warblers migrate to temperate woodlands in spring to nest and feed, but fly to warmer climates in the winter.

# TEMPERATE FORESTS OF THE WORLD

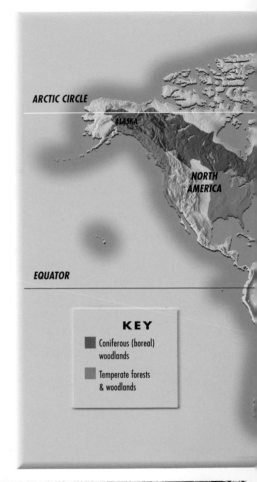

## EUCALYPTUS WOODLANDS

The eucalyptus woodlands of Australia contain an unusual collection of wildlife. The tree canopy (top layer of the trees) is fairly open, allowing sunlight through to the forest floor. The rain there falls mainly in the winter months.

Temperate woodlands have a temperate climate. Climate is measured by how much rain falls every year and what the average temperature is. In a temperate climate it gets warm in the summer and cool in the winter, but not as hot or cold as in other parts of the world. Temperate woodlands grow in areas that have an average temperature over 10°C (50°F) in the warmest months and 25 cm (10 inches) of rain a year. Coniferous forests grow across the top of North America, Europe and Asia, where temperatures fall below 0°C (32°F) for half the year and the growing season for plants lasts from one to three months. The rainfall in this area is between 25-50 cm (10-20 inches) every year. Deciduous forests grow further south where temperatures stay above 10°C (50°F) for half the year, rainfall is over 40 cm (16 inches) and the growing season is from three to seven months.

ARCTIC CIRCLE

ALASKA

NORTH AMERICA

EQUATOR

**KEY**

Coniferous (boreal) woodlands

Temperate forests & woodlands

## DECIDUOUS WOODLANDS

A quarter of the world's woodlands are made up of broadleaved deciduous trees, such as oak, birch, ash, beech and maple. To grow well, these trees need three times as many warm days as conifers do. In Europe, they grow south of the Baltic Sea and stretch into Russia. They also grow in eastern Asia, across China and Korea to Japan and in the middle and eastern states of America.

## BAMBOO FORESTS

Bamboos are giant grasses with woody stems. They grow in forests in parts of China and Japan. The hollow bamboo stems form a dense undergrowth where other plants cannot grow. The largest species of bamboo can grow to 40 metres (132 ft) in height. Most bamboos only produce seeds after 12-120 years, and only ever once in their lifetime. This causes problems for animals, such as the giant panda, that rely on these forests for food and shelter.

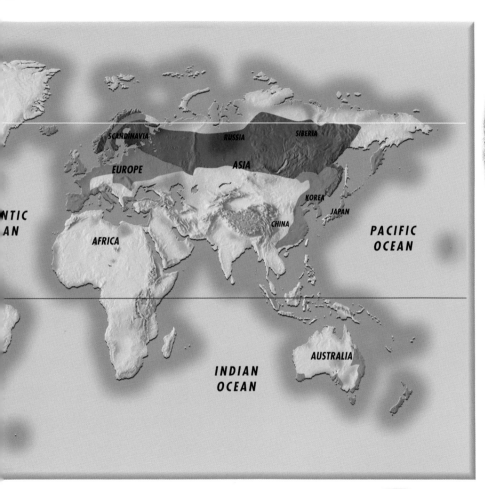

SCANDINAVIA
RUSSIA
SIBERIA
EUROPE
ASIA
KOREA
JAPAN
CHINA
PACIFIC OCEAN
NTIC AN
AFRICA
AUSTRALIA
INDIAN OCEAN

## CONIFEROUS WOODLANDS

Coniferous forests are made up of cone-bearing, or coniferous, trees such as spruces, hemlocks, pines and firs. The leaves of these trees are either needle-like or scale-like and most stay green all year round (evergreen). The great coniferous forests of the northern hemisphere make up the largest area of trees in the world. They are sometimes called boreal (northern) forests. From Alaska, they stretch to the Atlantic coast of North America. From one end to the other, the coniferous woodlands are 10,000 km (6,214 miles) long and 2,000 km (1,243 miles) wide.

## MONKEY PUZZLE FORESTS

The first monkey puzzle trees grew millions of years ago in the days of the dinosaurs. Now, they grow only in the Andes mountains of southeastern Chile. Also called Chilean pines, monkey puzzle trees grow to a height of 45 metres (150 ft). The needle-like leaves grow in spirals around stiff branches, which makes them hard to climb. Chilean woodlands are home to the Pehuenche people, who think of the trees as sacred. They do not cut the trees down but instead gather the seeds to grind into flour.

# CONIFEROUS FORESTS

## WHY NEEDLES?

Most conifers have long, thin, needle-shaped leaves on which snow does not easily settle and weigh down the branches. They contain very little sap, so there is little liquid to freeze. They tend to be dark in colour to absorb the maximum amount of heat from the sunshine. They don't lose much water because they are covered in a waxy surface that helps to retain water. Reducing water loss is important because roots cannot absorb water when the soil is frozen.

These forests are sometimes called the taiga, after a Russian word meaning 'dark and mysterious woodland'. The ancient needle-bearing trees of coniferous forests produce their seeds in cones. The trees appeared on Earth 300 million years ago, long before flowering plants. Coniferous trees are very good at deflecting the wind, so the inside of the woodland is often sheltered from even the fiercest winter blizzards. But this means very little light gets through to the forest floor and it is hard for anything to grow there among the dry layer of needles. Only a few plants, such as ferns, mosses, and small plants can survive there. Fungi do well because they do not need light to grow. Wild flowers and berry bushes, such as bilberry and juniper, thrive in clearings and natural gaps in the trees. Lakes form in hollows in the ground created by glaciers during the last ice age. The ground is often waterlogged because it takes a long time for water to evaporate. It also takes a long time for anything to decompose in the cold climate.

## WINTER SURVIVAL

During winter, some animals from the cold Arctic lands migrate south to shelter in conifer forests. Packs of wolves sometimes follow their prey, reindeer or caribou into the forests. Forest residents such as woodchucks and bats hibernate through the winter, while bears doze to save energy. Many birds migrate south to warmer climates and return in spring.

## FEEDING ON CONES

The tough, waxy needles of conifers are difficult to eat and most animals leave them alone. But the seeds in their cones are a vital source of nourishment. The crossbill has a crossed beak to help it prise the seeds from the cones. It may collect as many as a thousand seeds a day. A bigger bird called a nutcracker can crush cones with a bite to release the seeds.

## TREE SHAPES

Firs and spruces, such as these Colorado spruces (right), are shaped like cathedral spires. This shape encourages snow to slide easily from the downswept branches. If the snow were to build up, the branches might break under the weight.

## FIRE FORESTS

Fires are common in coniferous forests. The needles on the forest floor often ignite when a long, dry summer is followed by lightning strikes. Conifer trees tend to have thick bark to resist fires. The cones of some conifers, such as giant redwoods, only release their seeds during the heat of a forest fire. Pine trees in California need the fierce heat to make their seeds germinate (sprout). Because conifers grow close together, fires spread quickly and are hard to fight. Water is sometimes dropped on to them from helicopters.

## MAMMAL PREDATORS

Mammals are relatively scarce in northern forests, so predators, such as bobcats (left), sometimes have to cover vast distances to get food. Bobcats feed at night mainly on small rodents, such as lemmings and voles and birds. Their fur helps keep them warm.

# THE GIANT REDWOODS

Imagine walking through a forest so tall that the tree tops seem lost in the sky. Their red trunks are planted firmly in the ground and are so wide you could drive a car through a tunnel cut into them. These are the redwood trees of California, also called sequoias (pronounced 'si-koi-yas') after the American Indian scholar and leader Sequoyah. They are the oldest living things on Earth, standing tall after 3,000 years – forty human lifetimes. Their huge size is partly due to the fertile soil and humid conditions of the west coast of North America where the trees grow. A large network of roots take in enough moisture and nutrients to maintain a huge crown. One giant sequoia produces about 1,500-2,000 new cones a year and can still produce cones when it is thousands of years old.

## THICK SKIN

Redwood trees have reddish wood at the heart of the trunk and brownish-red coloured bark. The bark is thicker than that of any other species of tree on Earth and helps the trees to live for so long. Its bark may grow up to 76 cm (2.5 ft) thick in places. The bark is soft and does not easily catch alight, so the trees have some built-in fire protection.

## RATTLING SNAKE

The western diamondback is an American rattlesnake found on prairies, by streams and in redwood forests. If threatened, the snake raises its head and neck high above the ground in an S-curve. The rattling sound of the tail is designed to frighten enemies.

## EATING AND SLEEPING

American black bears are common in North American woodlands. They are active at night, and travel long distances in search of fruit, berries, nuts, roots and honey. In autumn, they gorge themselves on fruit to store enough body fat to last them through the winter. Bears do not hibernate but instead sleep in dens for 20-30 weeks of the year. Cubs are born in January or February and stay in the den with their mother until the spring.

## RED FLYER

Red bats roost in redwood trees during the day and emerge at night to feed on insects. This species of bat is unusual because it gives birth to three or four young instead of one or two. The female carries her young with her even though this combined body weight may exceed her own weight. Red bats migrate south in winter.

## TREE HOUSES

Carpenter ants live in colonies inside living sequoias as well as in logs and dead trees. They chew tunnels through the bark with their strong mandibles (mouthparts) to make chambers for their young. The ground underneath a nest is usually a mass of reddish sawdust. The colony chambers may be as long as 6 metres (20 ft). The tunnels do not really damage the tree but they may allow other insects and decay to enter. They also let air into the bark, which dries it out and makes it more likely to catch fire.

## WHY LEAVES FALL

Deciduous trees lose their leaves to help them survive the winter.

**WINTER**

*In winter there is not much sunlight, and water in the ground may become frozen. Without these two vital ingredients, trees cannot photosynthesise (make food), so they shut down.*

**SPRING/SUMMER**

*With spring rains and warmer, sunnier days, the trees come back to life. They grow new leaves and flowers.*

**AUTUMN**

*In autumn, the trees take nutrients from the leaves into the branches and trunks. The leaves change colour as they dry up and eventually fall off the tree.*

## VOLE ATTACK

Many rodents live in deciduous woods, including the bank voles of Europe and the jumping mice of North America. Bank voles are good climbers and often bite off tree bark to feed on the tree's living layer just beneath it. They may damage trees when food is scarce; but the field vole is a real danger. These voles sometimes chew a ring of bark right around the tree, which cuts off its food and water supply and kills it.

## LADY KILLERS

The wide, juicy leaves of deciduous trees make better meals than conifer needles and many insects and other animals eat them. But predators lurk among the leaves. Ladybirds and their larvae eat small insects such as aphids. During the Middle Ages, these beetles rid grapevines of insect pests and were dedicated to 'Our Lady', hence their common name.

## NEW ARRIVALS

Young animals, such as white-tailed deer fawns, are often born in spring when there is plenty to eat. They then have the summer to grow fit and strong before winter. The fawn's spotted coat helps to camouflage it among the trees; although all deer are difficult to see in woodlands because of their brown colours and the way they move so quietly through the trees.

# DECIDUOUS FORESTS

**W**arm summers, cool winters and steady rainfall throughout the year provide ideal conditions for deciduous trees such as oaks, beeches, chestnuts, maples and ashes. The North American forests have more species than in Europe and include aspen, linden, hickory, magnolia and buckeye as well as oak, beech and maple. There is plenty of water and sunshine available in the summer months. The broad leaves of the trees spread out to catch as much sunshine as possible. Deciduous forests are lighter and more open than conifer forests and more plants grow on the woodland floor. Yet they are still affected by the seasons. Spring and summer are times of plant growth and the birth of young animals. In the autumn, some trees lose their leaves and animals eat a lot to store food for the winter. Winter is a time of hibernation, migration, or a struggle to find food.

## TREE LEAVES

Deciduous tree leaves are usually wide and flat to help them catch the Sun's light energy. The leaves combine this with carbon dioxide from the air and water from the soil to make sugars, which are food for the tree. This process is called photosynthesis.

## WOODY WOODPECKER

The rapid drumming noise of a woodpecker's beak against a tree trunk is a familiar sound in deciduous woods. A woodpecker pecks a tree to dig out food or a nest, or to mark its territory and attract a mate. Woodpeckers have long, curved claws to cling to tree trunks. Their bills are sharply pointed to chisel into tree trunks and find insects, which they lick up with a long, sticky tongue. In some species, the tongue is as long as the bird's own body.

# TEMPERATE PLANTS

## GREEN CLIMBER

Ivy climbs up trees using special roots that sprout from the main stem. They are so fine they can grip into the tiniest crevice in the bark. The ivy sticks to the tree but there is no evidence that it takes any nourishment from it. Because ivy leaves are evergreen they can photosynthesise in winter. Ivy is one of the few plants that flowers in the autumn. It is pollinated by insects, such as flies and wasps, and develops berry-like fruits over the winter. Birds may eat the berries in spring and help to scatter the seeds.

Deciduous woodlands grow in three layers. The tallest trees such as oak, beech, maples and limes provide the upper layer, or canopy, of the forest. Shorter trees such as holly, willows and hazel grow in the middle. At the bottom are the flowering plants, ferns and mosses. To survive in the shade of the bigger trees, some plants climb up them, or grow on their branches to get nearer to the light. When the upper canopy of leaves falls in the autumn, more light reaches the evergreen plants in the middle and they continue to grow in winter. On the forest floor, plants either have large leaves to trap the light, or they feed on creatures – so they do not need light to make their own food. Coniferous forests tend to have two, rather than three layers of plant life because the trees cast so much shade. The damp soil of woodlands are ideal habitats for ferns and mosses which need moisture to reproduce. Fallen leaves and dead wood build up on the forest floor and provide rich nutrients for plants to recycle. Fungi are particularly important in the recycling process.

## LAYERS OF A WOODLAND

A woodland can be divided into three main layers.

**THE CANOPY**
*The highest level is made up of mature trees*

**THE SHRUB**
*The thick shrub level is made up of bushes, shrubs and young trees*

**THE FIELD LAYER**
*A carpet of flowers, herbs, ferns, and mosses*

*The woodland floor is covered with decaying leaves, fungi and plant debris.*

## FOREST FUNGI

Unlike green plants, fungi cannot make their own food. They absorb nutrients from plant sugars or other living things, both when they are alive and after they've died. The large amount of dead and decaying material in the woodlands is an ideal food source for fungi. Many of them live in partnership with the trees, taking some sugars from them but also helping the trees to absorb minerals from the soil.

## SPRINGING TO LIFE

Fire in this coniferous forest (right) has allowed more light to reach the forest floor, which has enabled the yellow heartleaf arnicas to grow over a large area. Many flowering plants, such as bluebells and wood sorrel, sprout in spring before the trees come into leaf and shade the woodland floor. They store food in bulbs, corms, tubers, or rhizomes under the ground, so are ready to grow quickly in spring.

## NESTING ORCHID

The bird's nest orchid is named for its thick, tangled mass of roots. The orchid does not have any green pigment, which plants need to photosynthesise. Instead the orchid obtains its nourishment from dead and decaying plant matter.

## FERN LIFE CYCLE

Ferns produce their spores in brown sacs on the underside of the leaves. The spores do not grow into new fern plants but into a tiny, heart-shaped structure called a prothallus which produces sperm and egg cells. A sperm cell has to meet with an egg cell before a new fern plant can develop. In winter, fern plants die back and their dead fronds (leaves) protect the growing tip of each plant during the most severe weather. In spring the plant grows back.

## BIG MOUTH

These tawny frogmouths (a type of nightjar bird) are well camouflaged by day. When they keep very still and upright, their speckled feathers look like broken branches. At night, the frogmouth comes down from its perch to catch beetles, centipedes, frogs and mice in its beak. The feathers at the base of the beak act like a cat's whiskers to help the bird find food or its way through the dark.

# EUCALYPTUS FORESTS

Australian eucalyptus forests are home to many different forms of wildlife, from brightly coloured birds to small furry mammals. The air in these forests is filled with the buzzing of insects and the strong sweet smells of eucalyptus leaves and acacia flowers. Dry bark hangs from the eucalyptus trunks in long, curly strips. Eventually it falls to the ground and mixes with fallen leaves, making the ground crunchy underfoot. The climate in these woodlands changes according to the season and rain falls mainly in the winter months. Rainwater collects in marshy pools, creating a habitat for frogs, snakes and water birds, such as ibises, pelicans, black swans and ducks. Many birds, like honeyeaters and lorikeets, and mammals, such as honey possums and bats, feed on the nectar and pollen in the eucalyptus trees and shrubs. Parrots use their strong bills to crack open seeds. Insects are also a source of food for other wildlife.

## FURRY PARACHUTE

Webs of furry skin between the front and back legs of a sugar glider spread out like a parachute when it jumps from tree to tree. Sugar gliders can glide for distances of 55 metres (180 ft) and land with a quiet plopping sound. They feed on insects, nectar, fruit and the sweet, sugary sap of wattle (acacia) and gum (eucalyptus) trees. Using their sharp front teeth they chew at the bark to reach the sap beneath it.

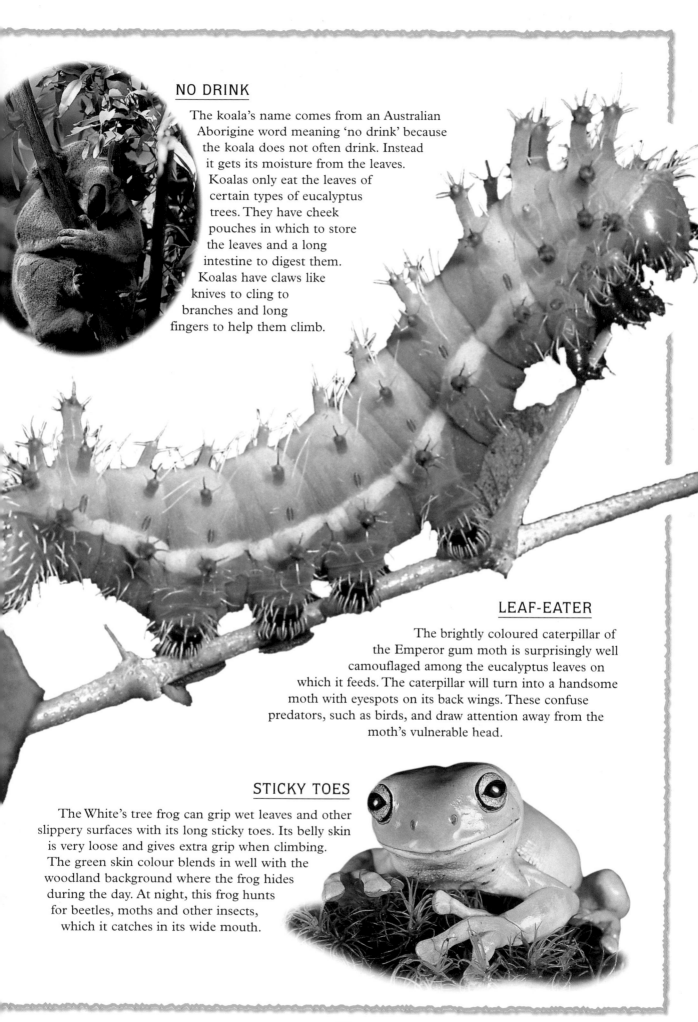

## NO DRINK

The koala's name comes from an Australian Aborigine word meaning 'no drink' because the koala does not often drink. Instead it gets its moisture from the leaves. Koalas only eat the leaves of certain types of eucalyptus trees. They have cheek pouches in which to store the leaves and a long intestine to digest them. Koalas have claws like knives to cling to branches and long fingers to help them climb.

## LEAF-EATER

The brightly coloured caterpillar of the Emperor gum moth is surprisingly well camouflaged among the eucalyptus leaves on which it feeds. The caterpillar will turn into a handsome moth with eyespots on its back wings. These confuse predators, such as birds, and draw attention away from the moth's vulnerable head.

## STICKY TOES

The White's tree frog can grip wet leaves and other slippery surfaces with its long sticky toes. Its belly skin is very loose and gives extra grip when climbing. The green skin colour blends in well with the woodland background where the frog hides during the day. At night, this frog hunts for beetles, moths and other insects, which it catches in its wide mouth.

**OAK LEAF SAP**

**OAK LEAF APHID**

**GREAT TIT**

**SPARROWHAWK**

*The juicy leaves of deciduous trees provide tasty snacks for many insects in the summer months. Small birds rely on these insects to feed themselves and their young. In turn, they are preyed upon by larger birds, such as sparrowhawks.*

# PREDATORS AND PREY

Woodland predators come in all shapes and sizes – from tiny spiders and beetles to huge owls and tigers. Swooping through the trees are birds such as owls, sparrowhawks, goshawks and crested hawks. Among the branches are martens, Australian western quolls, woodpeckers, pied flycatchers and solitary vireos. The northern shrike is a type of bird that has a hooked bill to catch frogs and grasshoppers in summer and finches and mice in winter. Larger hunters, such as the Siberian tiger, lynx, bobcat, red fox and wolverine, stalk their prey on the forest floor, often travelling large areas to find enough food. Lynx cover over 200 sq km (125 sq miles) when they are hunting. Prowling in the leaf litter on the ground are smaller hunters, such as salamanders, toads, snakes, shrews, wolf spiders, harvestmen, ground beetles and predatory fly larvae.

## CRAFTY COYOTE

Coyotes eat a lot of small mammals, including squirrels, rabbits and mice. Coyotes hunt small animals alone, but work together to bring down larger animals such as deer and Rocky Mountain sheep. Two or more coyotes may chase large prey for up to 400 metres (1,300 ft).

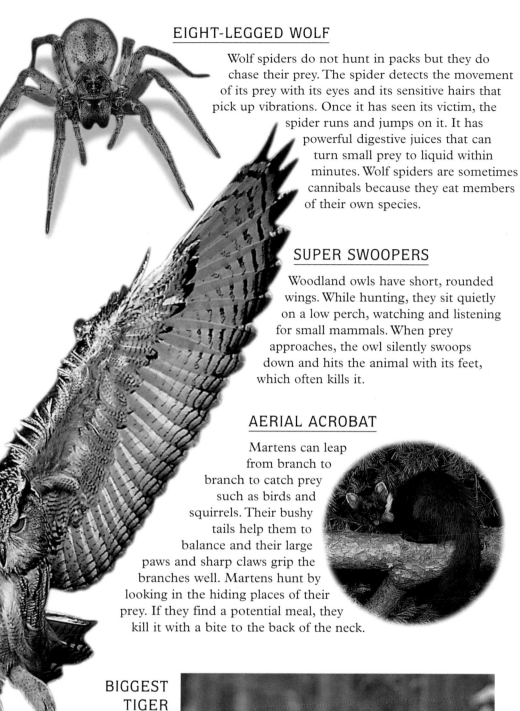

## EIGHT-LEGGED WOLF

Wolf spiders do not hunt in packs but they do chase their prey. The spider detects the movement of its prey with its eyes and its sensitive hairs that pick up vibrations. Once it has seen its victim, the spider runs and jumps on it. It has powerful digestive juices that can turn small prey to liquid within minutes. Wolf spiders are sometimes cannibals because they eat members of their own species.

## SUPER SWOOPERS

Woodland owls have short, rounded wings. While hunting, they sit quietly on a low perch, watching and listening for small mammals. When prey approaches, the owl silently swoops down and hits the animal with its feet, which often kills it.

## AERIAL ACROBAT

Martens can leap from branch to branch to catch prey such as birds and squirrels. Their bushy tails help them to balance and their large paws and sharp claws grip the branches well. Martens hunt by looking in the hiding places of their prey. If they find a potential meal, they kill it with a bite to the back of the neck.

## BIGGEST TIGER

The world's biggest cat, the Siberian tiger, hunts in the coniferous forests of northern Asia. Its enormous body and shaggy fur help it stay warm in the snow. Like all tigers, Siberian tigers hunt alone. They stalk their prey and then knock it over with the weight of their body or with their huge paws. A bite to the throat usually suffocates the prey. A Siberian tiger can eat over 35 kg (77 lbs) of meat in just one meal.

## CONIFER FOREST FOOD CHAIN

**FIR TREE**

**FUNGI**

**RED SQUIRREL**

**MARTEN**

*The fungi in conifer woods feed on dead and decaying trees. They are, in turn, eaten by herbivores, such as red squirrels. Carnivores, such as martens, prey on squirrels and other small animals.*

# DEFENCE

In the woodlands, animals are prey, predator, or both. As a result they have developed cunning methods of survival. Some, such as grass snakes and opossums, pretend to be dead, since most predators prefer to eat living prey, and leave them alone. Others are protected by sharp spines, armour or poisons. If the armour is on an animal's back, it rolls into a ball to protect its soft belly. Hedgehogs, echidnas and pill bugs (a type of woodlouse) do this to stop predators. If striped skunks are threatened, they stand on their heads and spray a horrible smelly liquid over their attacker. Lobster moth caterpillars squirt acid at their attackers; while puss moth caterpillars have huge fake eyes to make themselves look more dangerous. Other forms of defence include camouflage, hiding, or running away.

## CAMOUFLAGE

This Arsenura moth could easily be mistaken for just another leaf. It even has lines along its wings that look like the veins on leaves. In coniferous woodlands, many caterpillars avoid being seen by matching the colour and shape of the pine needles.

## TIGHTROPE TRICKS

At the slightest sign of danger, squirrels take to the trees, leaping from branch to branch, using their long tail for balance. Running up and down smooth tree trunks and standing on the thinnest twigs is easy for them. On the ground, squirrels often stop, sit upright and sniff the air. If they detect any possible danger, they use their tail to signal a warning to other squirrels.

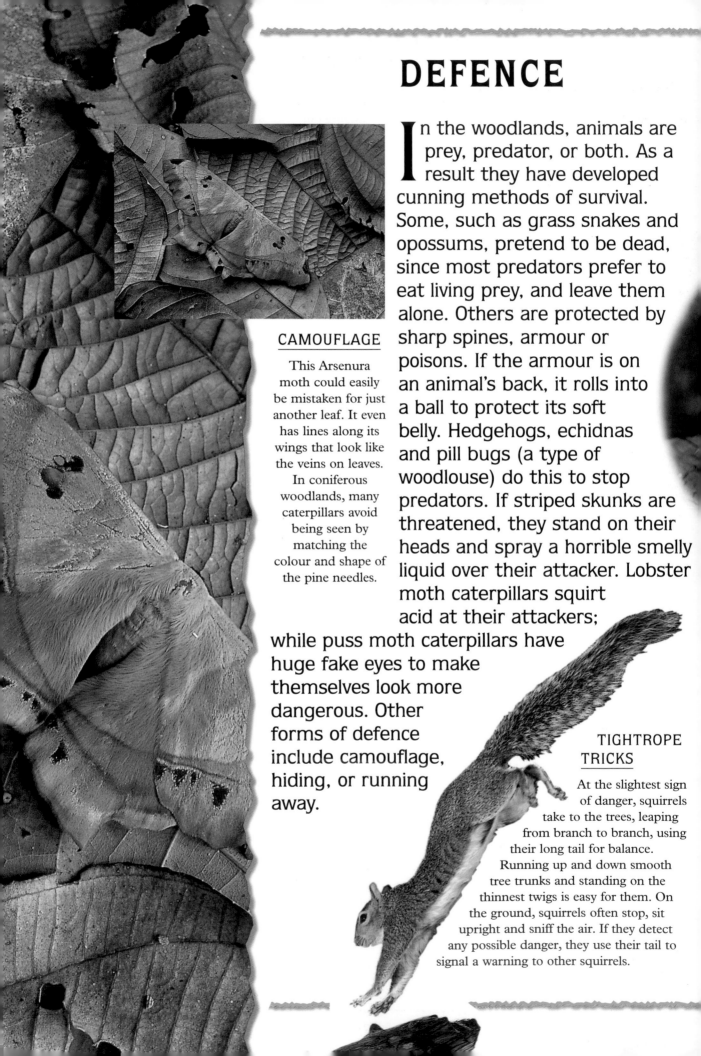

## DEAD OR ALIVE

When a North American opossum is under threat, it will open its mouth to show its 50 sharp teeth. Its other defence strategy is to 'play dead' by rolling over onto its back with its tongue hanging out. The opossum may stay in this trance-like state for hours.

## SPINY COAT

Australian echidnas, or spiny anteaters, use their sharp, spiny coats for protection. If threatened, they roll into a spiky ball. When disturbed in the open, they burrow straight down into ground, using their sharp claws and powerful bodies. Echidnas are clever too. They perform very well in scientific tests designed to test learning and memory. In some tests, they do better than cats, so are good at using their brains to avoid danger.

## BEWARE, POISON!

The brightly coloured spots and stripes of the fire salamander warn predators to leave it alone. Its skin secretes a poison that will irritate a predator's mouth and eyes, and is powerful enough to kill small mammals. The poison glands are located on the top of the head.

## GLUED TO THE SPOT

Even trees have their own defence. If a conifer tree is damaged, sticky resin oozes out of the cut to seal it like a plaster and protect the tree from attack by fungi and insects. This deer fly has been caught in the resin from a white pine tree. Insects from millions of years ago have been found preserved in amber (hardened resin).

# NIGHT-TIME ANIMALS

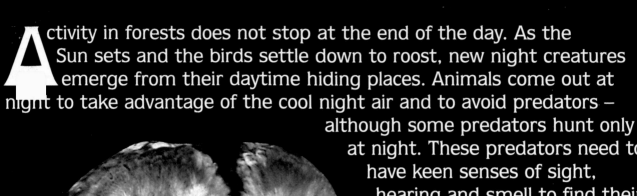

Activity in forests does not stop at the end of the day. As the Sun sets and the birds settle down to roost, new night creatures emerge from their daytime hiding places. Animals come out at night to take advantage of the cool night air and to avoid predators – although some predators hunt only at night. These predators need to have keen senses of sight, hearing and smell to find their way around and locate food. Some, such as badgers, have a special layer at the back of their eye to reflect as much light as possible into the eye. The long, sensitive whiskers of mice and other rodents help them feel their way in the dark. Nocturnal (night-time) animals are often well camouflaged to hide themselves from danger during the day.

## SILENT HUNTER

Tawny owls are hard to see during the day because their brown feathers blend in well with tree bark and leaves. At night, their keen hearing and silent flight make them excellent hunters. Fluffy, comb-like fringes on the feathers help make the owl's wings beat quietly. The velvety surface of the feathers muffles the sound of them brushing against each other and the air rushing between them.

## NIGHT-TIME RAMBLERS

Woodlice come out at night when woodlands are damp and cool. They often climb trees in search of lichens and algae to eat. Unlike insects, woodlice do not have a waterproof cuticle (body case), so they cannot afford to lose too much water. They instinctively move away from the light and come to rest in damp, dark places.

## HIDDEN MOTHS

Most woodland moths are well camouflaged to avoid being spotted by hunting birds. Their front wings look like the places they rest on during the day. This merveille du jour moth (left) is almost invisible when sitting on damp lichen-covered bark. Lappet and angleshades moths look like dead leaves. Green moths, such as the green silver lines or the emeralds, hide among fresh green leaves.

## BEETLE HUNTER

The greater horseshoe bat is slow in flight and not good at catching insects in the air. It flies and feeds quite low to the ground, swooping down on beetles, such as cockchafers in spring and dor beetles later in the year. It finds its way in the dark by producing high-pitched squeaks through its nose, while keeping its mouth shut. The echoes from this noise bounce back and inform the bat of the position of nearby objects and whether or not they are moving.

## MASTER DIGGERS

Eurasian badgers spend most of the day underground in their sett (the badger's home which is made up of tunnels and chambers). They dig this network of tunnels using their strong legs and claws. At dusk, a badger emerges from its sett for a night of hunting. Badgers are especially fond of earthworms but eat a variety of insects, rabbits, carrion (creatures already dead), and fruit. Shallow holes near a sett are where a badger has dug for food.

# COURTSHIP

In spring and autumn, forests are alive with the sounds of animal courtship. Sound is a useful means of communication as it can be easily heard even when the animals are hidden among the leaves and branches. Many birds migrate to the woodlands of the northern hemisphere in spring for courtship and nesting. The beautiful birdsong that fills these woodlands in spring is designed to attract a mate or claim a territory. Birds display their feathers to impress the mate.

Woodpeckers even use the trees as drums to send messages to potential mates or rivals. In the autumn, male deer roar out a challenge to their rivals and clash their antlers in spectacular fights over females. They grow new antlers every year. Insects are not usually as noisy as birds or mammals, relying more on scents and colours during courtship.

## FANTASTIC FAN

The male superb lyrebird has two broad tail feathers and a mass of long, silvery feathers at the back. The bird creates a small mound of soil with its feet, which he dances and sings on, to attract females for mating. During this courtship display, his long tail feathers spread out in a fan shape to impress a passing female.

## PANDA PARTNERS

Giant pandas live alone in the bamboo forests of southwest China. But in spring, the pandas look for a mate. When a female panda is ready to mate she lets the male panda know by leaving scent marks on logs and stones, and makes grunting noises. A male panda answers her calls and may roar to warn other males to keep away. A pair of mating pandas stay together for just a few days, then each goes its own way.

## FEATHERED DRUMMER

In spring, the ruffed grouse sits on a log and makes a drumming sound by beating his wings. The sound carries a long way through coniferous forests and helps to attract a female for mating. During his loud display, the male also spreads out his tail like a fan.

## CRICKET CALLS

In the dark woodland night, the male oak bush cricket drums his back legs against a leaf to attract a female. He then spreads his wings to make the drumming sounds louder. Females (shown left) pick up the drumming sounds of the males through 'ears' on their front legs and move towards the male of their choice. Both sexes have ears but only the males can drum.

## MATING MOTHS

Male cecropia, or robin moths, have tiny branches along their antennae. Tiny hairs along these branches catch the scent of female cecropia moths from far away. The female gives off a mating scent at night and the male follows its trail to find her.

# NESTS, EGGS & YOUNG

In a woodland, there are plenty of places to hide the young and keep them safe and warm. Even so, there is always competition for the best nesting sites. Birds sing loudly to claim the territory where they feed and breed. Tree holes make nest sites for birds such as owls and woodpeckers; while other birds and squirrels prefer to build nests high in the branches. Hollow trees make ideal roosting and hibernation sites for woodland bats. Other mammals nest among tree roots or in burrows hidden by dead leaves. Some small mammals, such as lemmings, breed very quickly. One female lemming may have 30-40 young in a season and some of those young may breed when they are only 19 days old. The forest is full of lemmings when the weather is good and food is plentiful. The trees also swarm with caterpillars and other insect young in spring and summer, providing a welcome supply of food for hungry birds. Some insects lay their eggs inside leaves or nuts or deep inside tree trunks. Wood is not very nutritious so those that eat it take a long time to grow.

## WOOD DRILL

Ichneumon flies make holes in pine trees to lay their eggs on wood wasp larvae. After hatching, the ichneumon larvae feed on the wood wasp larvae. The female's egg-laying tube, or ovipositor, is longer than her body to reach the wood wasp larvae hidden deep inside pine trees. She can drill a hole 3 cm (1¼ inches) into the pine tree in under 20 minutes.

## BABY CARRIER

Female red-necked pademelons (a type of marsupial) are smaller than the males. This wallaby (left), found in Australia, has four teats in a pouch on the front of her body. She rears a single young, which stays in the pouch for about 26 weeks. It is tiny and undeveloped when it is born but is kept warm, safe, and fed inside the pouch.

## CUTE CUBS

Brown bears mate in May or June and the cubs are born 10 months later in the winter. The mother gives birth in a cave, hollow tree or other sheltered spot. She and the cubs do not venture out of the den until April or June. The cubs weigh only 350-400g (12-14 lbs) when born. They have hardly any fur and are quite helpless but grow fast on their mother's rich milk. Mother and cubs stay together for 1½–4½ years. The age at which the female gives birth and the size of her litter depends on the quality of her diet.

## VOLE CONTROL

Great grey owls feed almost entirely on voles. The number of voles tends to increase over a period of five or six years and then falls suddenly. When there are lots of voles, the well-fed owls produce bigger and bigger clutches (a group of owl eggs). Eventually, they may lay seven, eight, or even nine eggs in a clutch. In years when there are few voles, great grey owls may lay only one or two eggs. If the owls' face starvation, they leave the northern forests to travel south in search of food.

## CAMOUFLAGE COAT

Female wild boars give birth to a litter of up to 10 young in spring or early summer. The young have stripes to help camouflage them in the light and shade of the woodland. One or two adult sows (females) live together with their young of various ages. Adult males live alone or in small bachelor groups that stay close to the females and their young.

# LIVING TOGETHER

Living together in social groups helps the survival of many woodland animals, such as deer, wild boar, bats and wood ants. The individuals in a group help each other to spot danger, find food and rear the young. In mammal societies, adults pass on survival skills to younger members of the group. Insect societies are highly organised, with different individuals carrying out different tasks, such as gathering food or guarding the nest. Some birds, such as American red-cockaded woodpeckers, live in groups where only one pair nests – the others take it in turns to guard the nest hole. They may also help to feed the young. Often, two different types of creatures help each other survive in woodlands. For example, ambrosia beetles farm fungi in their tunnels and eat the fruiting bodies. The fungi feed on the beetle droppings, converting any undigested wood into a form the beetle can eat.

## GALL MAKERS

Strange growths called galls develop on many woodland plants. Most are caused by gall wasps, but others by beetles, flies and mites which lay their eggs somewhere in the leaves or twigs. When the larvae hatch out, their presence stimulates the surrounding plant tissue to grow into a variety of oddly-shaped galls. Each gall contains one or more developing larvae. In some, the adult insect hatches out in the summer. In others, the gall turns brown and the larvae inside hibernates through the winter. There will often be other insects within the gall, some of them parasites. The oak apple gall has been known to house 75 different species of insect as well as the gall wasp grub.

## LAZY CUCKOOS

The female cuckoo lays her eggs in other birds' nests, often with colours and markings to match those of the bird whose nest it is. When the cuckoo chick hatches after 12 days, it quickly gets rid of the other eggs and chicks, so it can have all the food. The baby cuckoo puts each egg and chick into its hollowed-out back, hoists itself over the rim of the nest, and tips them out!

## RED DEER

Red deer are sociable animals but the adult males and females live apart except during the October rut (mating season). One herd is made up of a mature female, her female relatives and their young. Herds of adult males have a hierarchy, which puts each male in a different position of importance. The buck with the biggest antlers is the dominant male but he loses his place in the hierarchy when he loses his antlers in March or June. The hierarchy is only re-established when all the males grow new antlers the next year.

## WOOD ANTS

Colonies of wood ants may contain up to 500,000 ants. The ants search for insects, such as beetles (right), to take back to their nest. A big colony can eat up to 100,000 insects and larvae in a day. The nest is made of a huge pile of pine needles, small sticks and other debris and can be 1.5 metres (5 ft) high and 3 metres (10 ft) in diameter. In the earth below the nest is a network of corridors and chambers. In most nests there are several large queen ants laying eggs, with workers cleaning and feeding the larvae. Guard ants squirt enemies with acid. On warm spring and summer days, thousands of winged males and females emerge from the nest. After mating, the fertilised queens fly off to create a new colony.

## A SIMPLE ANTS' NEST

*An entrance to the nest can be closed in cold or rainy weather, or to control nest temperature.*

*Rubbish chamber*

*Food chamber*

*Larvae spin cocoons and pupate inside them.*

*Workers move pupae around to keep them at an even temperature.*

*Eggs hatch into larvae. Workers clean and feed them.*

*Queen lays eggs.*

*Queen's Chamber. She is larger than the workers.*

# PEOPLE & TEMPERATE FORESTS

## FROM WOODS TO FARMS

Many woodlands in Europe and North America have been reduced to small clumps of trees in the middle of fields. Trees are slow to grow and hard to harvest. Few farmers can afford to wait over 50 years to make money from a wood crop. Woodlands tend to survive on steeply sloping land that is unsuitable for ploughing, or where people still use trees for firewood and in other traditional ways.

For thousands of years humans were scared of forests because predatory animals lived in them. But humans also relied on the forests for food and the natural materials found in them. Many traditional peoples have lived entirely from woodlands, respecting the trees and other living creatures. They took only what they needed and were themselves part of a balanced ecosystem. Most of these peoples no longer live in this way and many of the woodlands have been destroyed. Nowadays, woodlands provide products rather than shelter for people. Timber is harvested or grown in special plantations. Cork is harvested from the bark of cork oak trees in Mediterranean lands. It can be stripped off about every ten years without damaging the trees. Fruit and fungi are also harvested in many countries, such as France. But many of us enjoy woodlands for activities such as cycling, walking and birdwatching.

## WOODEN HOUSES

Nowadays, forests are used mainly to provide timber for buildings and furniture. This log cabin in an American aspen forest is constructed entirely of wood, but even brick or stone houses usually have wooden frameworks and roof supports. A lot of building timber and wood for making paper is grown in renewable plantations. Fast-growing tree species are planted in straight lines to make them easier and faster to harvest. Plantations are not as rich in wildlife as natural woodlands.

## TRUFFLE HUNTING

Pigs and dogs are trained to sniff out edible truffles, the fruit of a fungus that grows next to tree roots, at depths of about 30 cm (12 inches). Truffles range in size from as small as a pea to as big as an orange, and many are considered a delicacy, especially the black Perigord truffle. The truffle industry is important in France.

## WOOD TRANSPORT

Trees are bulky and difficult to move so they were traditionally transported along rivers. The areas most heavily logged were those with large rivers. The woodlands that were not near the river used to survive untouched. Pulpmills like this one, are often located at the mouth of a river, especially where it enters a lake, which can be used to store floating logs. Trucks now transport logs, so woodlands far from rivers are being logged.

## TOTEM POLES

This Kwakiutl chief from Canada is wearing an eagle headdress. The Kwakiutl people built villages of wooden houses and were famous for their arts, particularly their totem poles. Carved from trees, the poles show animals that have a special relationship with the spirits and way of life of the community. If the tribe shows an animal on the totem, then it will be one that the tribe will not eat. Through such symbols and beliefs, many tribes express their relationship with the environment.

# PROTECTING TEMPERATE FORESTS

## BISON REFUGE

The great Bialowieza forest in Poland is one of the last wild woodlands left in Europe. European bison became extinct in the wild in 1919 but were re-introduced into the Bialowieza Primeval forest from zoo collections. This bison at a breeding centre in Poland will eventually be released into the forest.

Temperate woodlands are vital to the survival of the Earth. They affect the balance of water and gases in the atmosphere, prevent soil erosion, and are home to a wide variety of wildlife. But only a fraction of Europe's original temperate forests remain and the great northern coniferous woodlands are disappearing fast, either being cleared for timber or to make way for houses and farms. Pollution, such as acid rain, has taken its toll, particularly on the coniferous forests. Fires and fungus diseases also cause a lot of damage. More could be done to save the remaining temperate woodlands and use them sustainably: cork can be harvested; trees can be coppiced (cut so they grow again); new trees can be planted to replace those cut down; and pollution can be reduced.

## FOREST FIRES

Natural forest fires in small areas are essential for seeds to spread and to create open spaces where new trees can grow. But large-scale fires, often carelessly started by cigarettes or campfires, are hard to control and cause terrible destruction to trees and the wildlife. People who use woodlands need to be aware of the fire risk.

## SAVE THE PANDA

There are probably around 1,000 giant pandas left in the wild. They are difficult to breed in captivity, so this female is being artificially inseminated (made pregnant) at a breeding centre in China. She may have one or two cubs. Pandas were more common hundreds of years ago when there were bamboo forests all over China. But they were cut down to build villages and so that rice could be grown on the land. People also hunted pandas for their skins. It is now against the law to hunt pandas. They are protected in reserves but are still an endangered species.

## COPPICING

One way of harvesting timber sustainably is to cut the trees down to a stump. Several new shoots grow from the cut stump instead of one trunk and can be harvested several years later. Old coppiced trees which have not been harvested recently have several cut trunks rather than one. Hazel and sweet chestnut are suitable trees for harvesting like this. Coppiced woodlands are light and open, which encourages the growth of flowering plants on the woodland floor.

## FUTURE WOODS

A person walking along a nature trail in a woodland forest will quickly notice the importance of woodlands to wildlife. Woodlands will only survive in the future if we understand more about the way they work, appreciate how and why they are threatened, and do more to preserve existing woodlands and create new ones. Creating more National Parks would preserve important areas.

## ACID RAIN

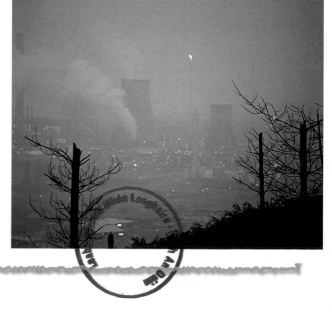

Vast areas of temperate woodlands in Europe and North America are badly affected by acid rain. It contains more acid than is natural because of the huge volume of smoke and chemical fumes released into the air by motor vehicles and power stations. Acid rain caused in one country is often blown by the wind over another. Trees in southern Canada are being killed by acid rain created in northern USA. Pollution from most of western Europe is killing trees in southern Norway and Sweden. Acid rain is lethal for coniferous forests which already have acid soils. By releasing aluminium into the soil, acid rain poisons tree roots.

# GLOSSARY

**Coppicing** A method of cutting trees off at the stump to allow new shoots to grow from it.

**Deciduous** A tree or plant that loses its leaves annually when the season changes, usually in the Autumn.

**Ecosystem** A community of living and non-living things depending on each other for mutual survival.

**Evergreen** A type of tree or plant that keeps its leaves the whole year round.

**Germinate** The process where seeds or spores sprout from a plant and begin to grow.

**Growing season** The period of each year when plants grow, determined by location, climate, rainfall and daylight.

**Hibernation** The time when some animals go into a deep sleep for the winter, living off the fat stored in their bodies.

**Pollination** The process where pollen is carried to a flower's reproductive organs (usually by insects) allowing the flower to produce seeds.

**Photosynthesis** The process used by green plants to make food from light energy, carbon dioxide and water.

**Temperate** A type of climate that does not suffer from extreme temperatures and usually has the same length summers as winters.

## ACKNOWLEDGEMENTS

We would like to thank: Helen Wire and Elizabeth Wiggans for their assistance. Artwork by Peter Bull Art Studio.

Copyright © 2009 ticktock Entertainment Ltd

First published in Great Britain by ticktock Media Ltd, The Old Sawmill, 103 Goods Station Road, Tunbridge Wells, Kent TN1 2DP, Great Britain

All rights reserved. No part of this publication may be reproduced, stored in a retrieval system, or transmitted in any form or by any means electronic, mechanical, photocopying, recording or otherwise, without prior written permission of the copyright owner.

A CIP catalogue record for this book is available from the British Library.

ISBN 978 1 84898 005 1 (paperback)

ISBN 978 1 84898 050 1 (hardback)

Picture research by Image Select. Printed in China.

Picture Credits: t=top, b=bottom, c=centre, l=left, r=right, OFC=outside front cover, OBC=outside back cover, IFC=inside front cover

Image Bank; 22c. Oxford Scientific Films; 2/3ct, 3tr, 3br, 4br, 5cb, 7tl, 7cr, 8/9cb, 9tr, 9cr, 10ct, 11br & OBCbl, 12tl, 12/13c, 13b, 14tl, 14bl, 14/15c, 17c, 17tl, 18cb, 18/19c, 19r, 19tl, 19bl, 20l, 20/21, 21c & OBCbr, 21tr, 21bl, 22tl, 22/23b, 23t, 24b, 24tl, 25c, 26c, 26bl, 27tr, 29tr, 30c, 30/31ct. Shutterstock; OFC. Still Pictures; 11tr. Tony Stone; IFC & 4tl, 32 & 6/7b, 2l, 23/cb, 4br, 5cr, 5tl, 6tl, 6/7c, 6/7b, 8l, 9tl, 10l, 10/11ct, 10/11cb, 12r, 13t, 15tl 15br, 15bl, 16bl, 16/17c, 17cb, 18l & (inset), 23r, 25tr, 25b, 26/27ct, 28tl, 28bl, 28/29, 29cr, 30l, 30/311c, 31br.

Every effort has been made to trace the copyright holders and we apologise in advance for any unintentional omissions. We would be pleased to insert the appropriate acknowledgement in any subsequent edition of this publication.